AF285127

THE AFR🪐FUTURIST COLORING BOOK

VOL. 2
THE DREAMSCAPE EDITION

FORD KELLY

Bibliografische Information der Deutschen Nationalbibliothek: Die Deutsche Nationalbibliothek verzeichnet diese Publikation in der Deutschen Nationalbibliografie; detaillierte bibliografische Daten sind im Internet über dnb.dnb.de abrufbar.

Text, Layout and Illustrations: Ford Kelly

Herstellung und Verlag: BoD – Books on Demand, Norderstedt

ISBN: 978-3-7543-4313-5 (The Afrofuturist Coloring Book Vol. 2: The Dreamscape Edition)

Disclaimer: Dies ist ein Werk der Afrofiction. Figuren, Orte und Szenarien sind entweder Produkte der Fantasie des Künstler:in oder fiktiv. Jegliche Ähnlichkeit mit lebenden oder von uns gegangenen Personen, Ereignissen oder Szenarien entspringt dem Zufall. Sollte eines dieser Bilder in irgendeiner Weise der Zukunft entsprechen, wäre auch dies ein großer Zufall.

THE
AFR⬤FUTURIST
COLORING BOOK

VOL. 2
THE DREAMSCAPE EDITION

FORD KELLY

Afrofuturism plays with the
past, present and the future. Time is
adapted and augmented to reconsider how our
realities and identities are constructed. Afrofuturism
allows adventures to come alive within Africa and the
Diaspora. Recognising the endless possibilities within the
Dreamscape to travel. It explores our connection to mysticism, nature,
gender non-conformity, myths and metaphors.

The Dreamscape is an integral part of Afrofuturism. It allows endless
possibilities to re-imagine a future where Black people have not only
survived but have thrived. One where Black queer and trans people also have
central roles. A future where Myths and legends are merged into new realms.
Where Representation can be explored and reexamined.

The Afrofuturist Coloring Book - Volume Two, The Dreamscape edition is
the second Coloring book in the series. It features different Dreamscape
motivational prompts as well as 26 illustrated drawings with images
of Afro-Cyborgs, Witches, Warriors, Mystic Beings and much more!
Pick your medium of choice, whether crayons or coloring
pencils and let the pages inspire you.

Coloring books are for all ages to enjoy!

Have fun!

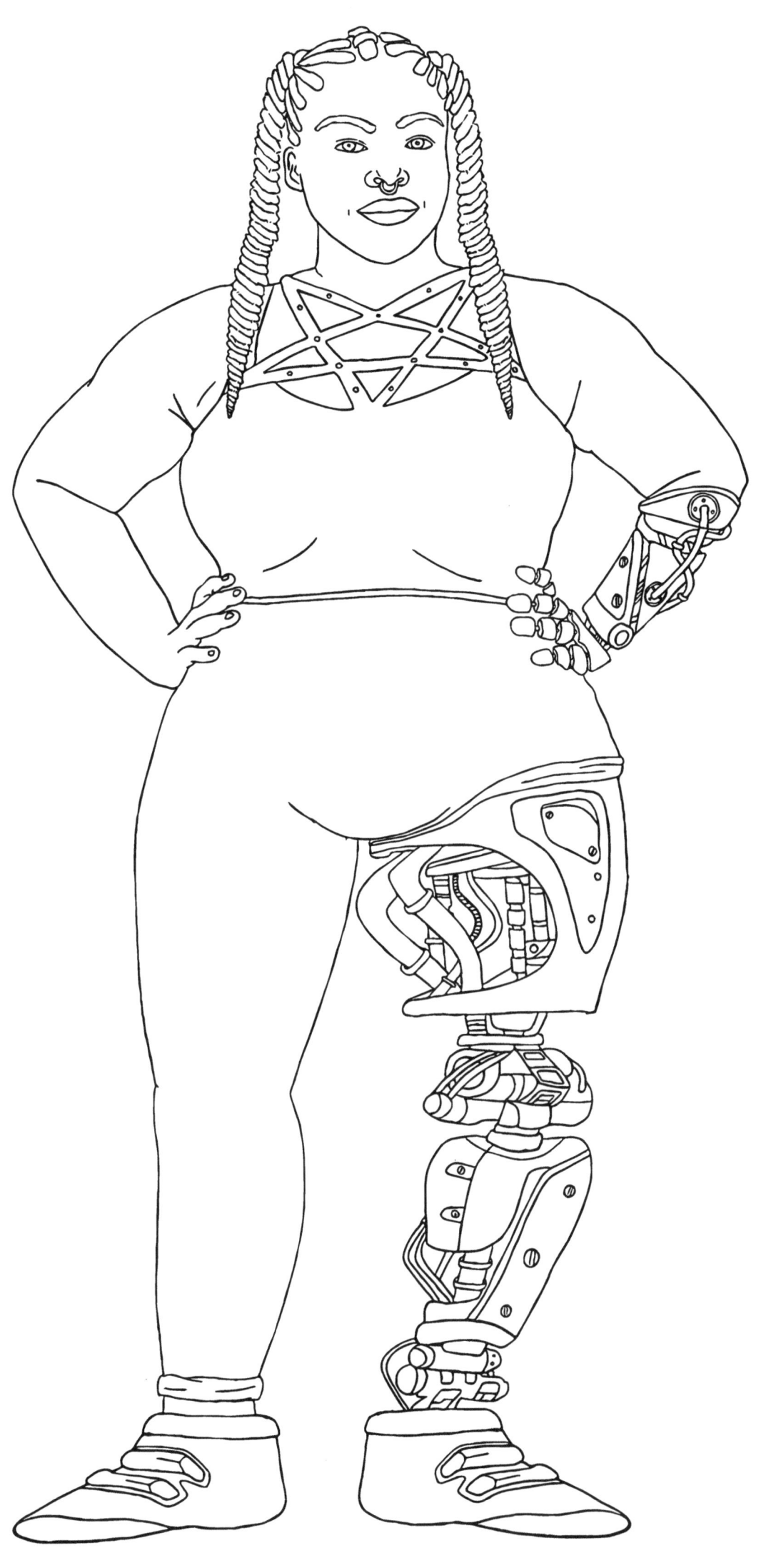

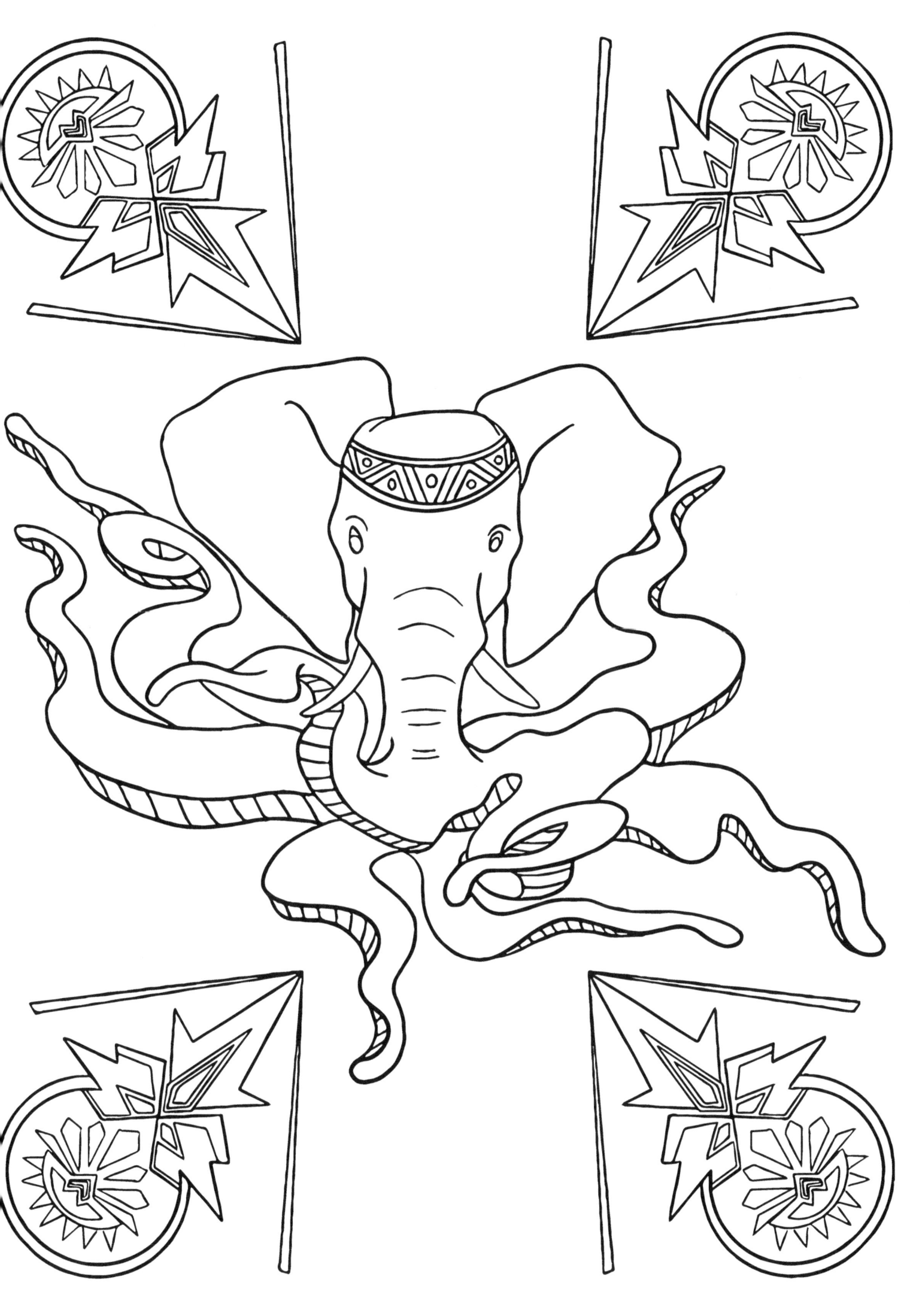

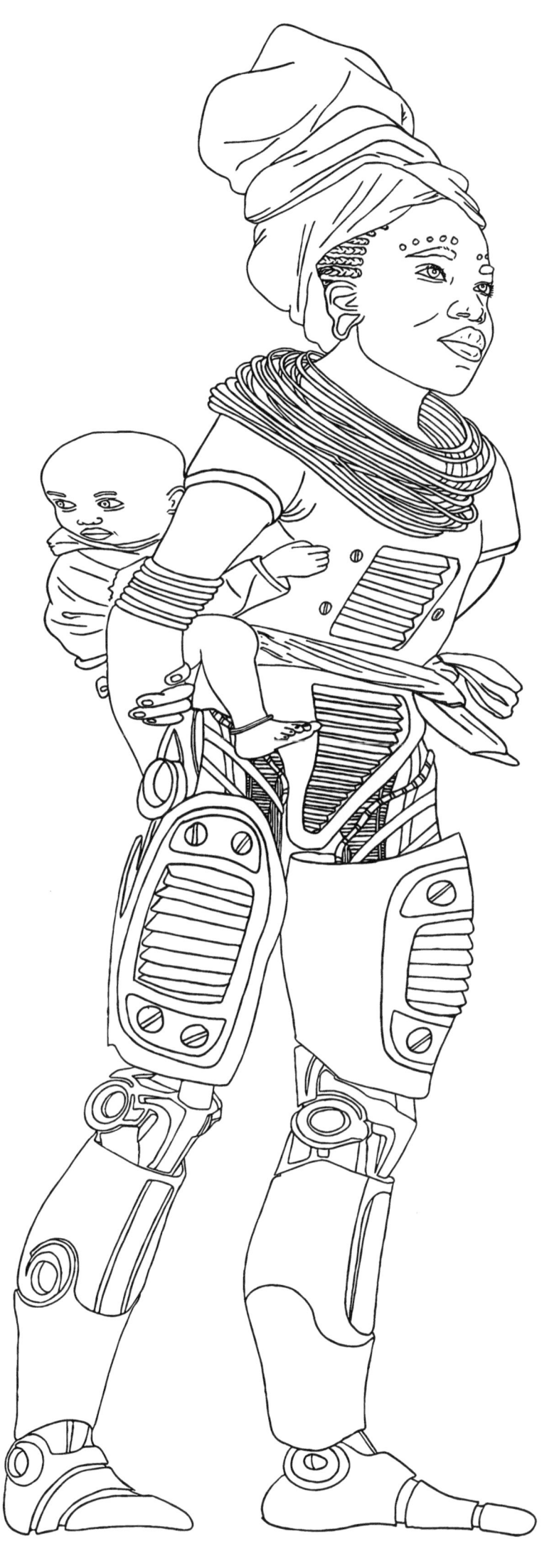

AFROFUTURIST INSPIRED *DREAMSCAPE PROMPTS.

How would you shape your Dreamscape for today, this week or this month?

What's one Dreamscape that makes you feel the most inspired? Describe this space in detail.

What intergenerational wisdom have you learned from your surroundings?

How can you deprogram your view on productivity today?

How can your imagination shift your reality today?

If your Ancestors were to ask you what makes your heart sing, how would you respond?

Write a letter to yourself now, as your future self.

What possibilities has the universe gifted you today or this week?

How do you recognise your authentic self?

What self identity are you still experimenting with?

What ideas have changed inside you recently?

What magic do you recognise in yourself?

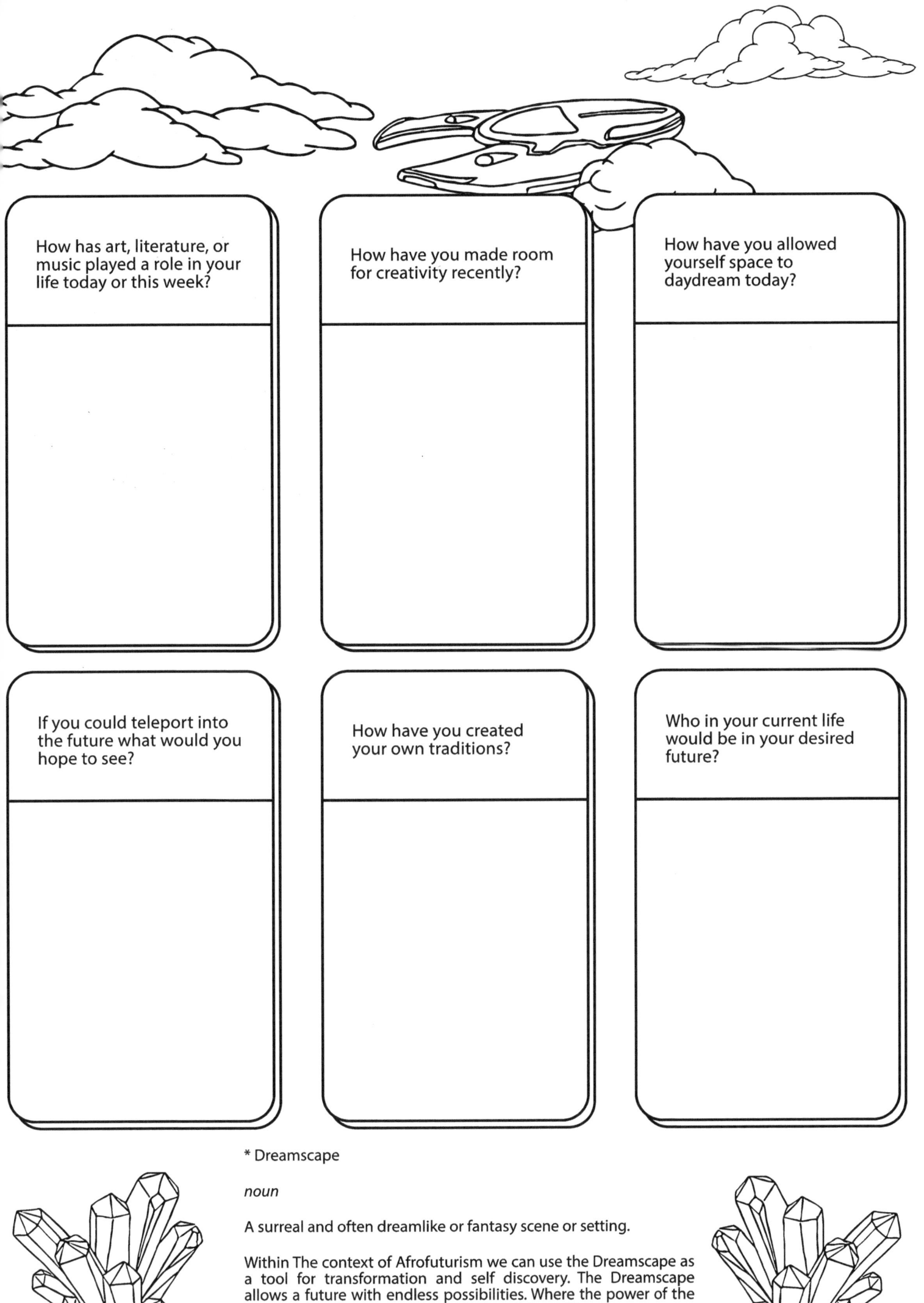

How has art, literature, or music played a role in your life today or this week?

How have you made room for creativity recently?

How have you allowed yourself space to daydream today?

If you could teleport into the future what would you hope to see?

How have you created your own traditions?

Who in your current life would be in your desired future?

* Dreamscape

noun

A surreal and often dreamlike or fantasy scene or setting.

Within The context of Afrofuturism we can use the Dreamscape as a tool for transformation and self discovery. The Dreamscape allows a future with endless possibilities. Where the power of the imagination allows us to dream fantasy into reality.